Learn To speak Haitian Creole

CHECK OUT OUR WEBSITE AND CHECK OUT OUR OTHER BOOK

© Copyright 2017 - All rights reserved.

The contents of this book may not be reproduced, duplicated or transmitted without direct written permission from the author.

Under no circumstances will any legal responsibility or blame be held against the publisher for any reparation, damages, or monetary loss due to the information herein, either directly or indirectly.

Legal Notice:

This book is copyright protected. This is only for personal use. You cannot amend, distribute, sell, use, quote or paraphrase any part or the content within this book without the consent of the author.

Disclaimer Notice:

Please note the information contained within this document is for educational and entertainment purposes only. Every attempt has been made to provide accurate, up to date and reliable complete information. No warranties of any kind are expressed or implied. Readers acknowledge that the author is not engaging in the rendering of legal, financial, medical or professional advice. The content of this book has been derived from various sources. Please consult a licensed professional before attempting any techniques outlined in this book.

By reading this document, the reader agrees that under no circumstances are is the author responsible for any losses, direct or indirect, which are incurred as a result of the use of information contained within this document, including, but not limited to, — errors, omissions, or inaccuracies.

Table of Contents

Introduction

Chapter 1: History of Haiti

Chapter 2: Haiti and France

Chapter 3: History of Haitian Creole

Chapter 4: Alphabets in Creole and French

Chapter 5: Cardinal and Ordinal Numbers in French and Creole

Chapter 6: Months of the Year, Days of the Week, and Time

Chapter 7: Useful Words and Phrases

Chapter 8: Some More Useful Phrases

Conclusion

Introduction

Haiti forms the western part of the island of Hispaniola. It occupies about one-third of the Hispaniola Island. About one-third of Hispaniola is Haiti and the balance is the Dominican Republic. Haiti is comparable in size to Maryland, US, and nearly 2/3rds of the country is mountainous and the rest is full of verdant beautiful valleys, small plains and extensive plateau lands. The largest city and the capital of Haiti is Port-au-Prince.

Haiti means 'mountainous country.' This meaning is derived from the language of the Taino Indians, the original inhabitants of the island before colonization by European countries. While Creole is the lingua franca and the official language in Haiti, its close neighbor, the Dominican Republic is predominantly Spanish.

Haiti is part of the Caribbean Islands, the more famous ones of which are Puerto Rico, Cuba and Jamaica. Haiti is prone to earthquakes and a really huge one hit the country in January 2010 in which about 300,000 people died and numerous others were injured. In fact, the Haitian people are still recovering from the devastating effects of the 2010 earthquake.

Let me give you some statistics at this point in time. The October 1989, an earthquake in San Francisco measuring 6.9 on the Richter scale resulted in 63 casualties. The February 2010 earthquake in Chile measuring 8.8 on the Richter scale and resulted in over 700 casualties. The January 2010 earthquake that struck Haiti measuring 7.0 on the Richter scale (similar to the intensity of the 1989 San Francisco earthquake) and resulted in nearly 300,000 people casualties! Why is there this astounding difference in casualty numbers between disasters in Haiti and other places on this planet? Isn't it necessary to know why?

Most experts opine that the reason for Haiti to remain poor, backward and ignored is due to racism. Most developed and rich nations have a negative connotation about Blacks and their abilities for advancement and upliftment, the experts believe. Hence, many Haitian experts and activities attribute this lack of awareness and ignorance about Haiti across the world to racism.

The island of Haiti is beautiful and yet is unfortunately ignored by many of the developed and rich nations of the world. This is sad indeed considering the fact that history tells us that many of today's rich countries were dependent on the resources of this wonderful country to build its own riches and wealthy.

Moreover, there are historically astounding facts about Haiti which are forgotten today. The first cathedral was built in Haiti. The first European University was built in Haiti. There was a time when Haiti was an extremely wealthy European colony. The unfortunate thing that happened to Haiti was the systematic draining of the natural resources of the country leaving it quite unable to be self-sufficient now.

The largest resource that was drained in Haiti was its people. There was a time when Haitians were robust and strong enough to work tirelessly in the fields and plantations of European settlers. Today, their condition is very sad. Nearly 50% of the children are malnourished and nearly 1/3rd of the children will die by the time they are five years!

While I will be talking about the history of Haiti in the coming chapters, my book is dedicated to the beautiful language of Haitian Creole. Despite having its roots firmly established in French, Creole has a uniqueness that is hard to miss. The commonality between French and Creole cannot be disputed and yet the individualism of Creole is there for all to see.

Allow me to tell you how I have structured this book. The first three chapters are dedicated to the history of Haiti, the love-hate relationship between Haiti and France, and the history of Haitian Creole. I believe knowing, understanding and appreciating the origins and histories of any element will help us in learning the language better while making the learning process wholesome.

I have used one chapter to explain (and, perhaps, add some extra tidbits wherever appropriate) the Creole and French aspects of the following elements:

- Alphabets
- Numbers
- Months of the year
- Time and days of the week
- Some useful phrases

I have explained the nuances of both the languages in the same chapter so as to make it easy for you to compare and contrast. So, go ahead and learn to speak both French and Creole.

Chapter 1: History of Haiti

To reiterate what was said in the Introduction chapter of this book, Haiti occupies about 1/3rd of the island of Hispaniola on the western side and its eastern neighbor is the Dominican Republic. The recorded history of Haiti coincides with the landing of Christopher Columbus on December 6, 1492, on the coast of the island of Hispaniola. Before coming to post-Columbus era, let us go back a little about the early history of Hispaniola

Early history of Hispaniola

Before the time of Columbus, Haiti was occupied by the Carib and Arawak (also called the Taino) Indians. Although it is now very difficult to know the exact population of these tribes that lived there, it is quite clear that they were very large in number and historians put a figure of about half a million as a reasonable estimate.

These people are known to have lived a simple and contented life, living off farming and fishing produce. History says that by a twist of bad luck, these Taino Indians made friends with the Spanish and gave them gold jewelry as gifts. The sight of gold drove the greed of the Spanish who erroneously thought that Haiti was an island of gold. They wanted to take as much gold as they could. In a bid to capture it, the Spanish continuously raided the islands and suppressed the Taino Indians.

On realizing that gold was not available on the island (after a few disastrous years of violent raids and deaths), the Spanish converted it into a bread basket growing and producing food for their Conquistadors. The Taino Indians were forced to labor in the fields for the Spanish people. The Taino Indians contracted European diseases and the situation of forced slavery did not bode well for them and soon, they were decimated.

Post-Columbus Era in Haiti

On landing there, Columbus found a Taino Indian kingdom ruled by a cacique or the Taino Indian chief. The indigenous tribes of the region were slowly being terminated and by the time the French colonized Hispaniola in the seventeenth century, the indigenous were almost annihilated completely.

Consequently, for the sake of hard labor, people from Africa were kidnapped and brought here as slaves. Slave labor was an essential need because the colonizers could not do all the hard work such as work on the extensive farms and coffee plantations. These kidnapped slaves were mostly from West Africa. In the 18th century, Haiti was considered to be the wealthiest French colonies and was given the moniker, "Pearl of the Antilles."

I beg to digress here for a moment to dwell on something quite deep and important when it comes to Haitians fight for independence. Many people like to believe that the revolution in Haiti did not start in what is popularly known to be around 1791. Even historians like Prof. Bayyinah Bello believe strongly that the revolution in Haiti started way back when the first slave was kidnapped from Africa to be traded as slaves.

She opines that the seed of revolution started from the time white hands were laid on a free Black and forced him into a boat. Her emotion to the cause of the Haiti revolution is palpable and, infectious even, as she describes how each of the free men would have fought all the way to the boat waiting to take them away from their homes, how they would have fought and, perhaps, given up their lives on the boat, and how they would have continued this fight relentlessly even after reaching new shores. This fight, she says, continued and peaked during the Haitian revolution (more about this too in the next two chapters). Let us move on to the history of Haiti.

During the period 1791-1804, the slave population in Haiti revolted against the French colonizers and their exploitation and as a result of this revolution, Napoleon Bonaparte was compelled to sell Louisiana to the US in 1803 resulting in an unprecedented expansion of US territories. Haitians obtained independence from their French colonizers in 1803 after which the country was renamed to Haiti from the French-given name of Saint Dominique. Haiti has its roots Ayiti, the Creole version.

The 2010 earthquake left Haiti battered and completely disheveled. An estimated 300,000 were killed, nearly 200,000 injured, and many more left homeless. The 2010 earthquake left a trail of disaster that is still evident today as people are struggling to cope with poverty, malnourishment, high child mortality rate, and more such problems. The 2010 earthquake ravaged the country mercilessly and is considered to be the worst catastrophe in the history of the country.

Haiti's history is complex and fascinating replete with stories of revolt, instability, victory, and valorous deeds. But the foundation of Haiti and its people lies in its resilience. Despite the backlash of slavery, the backlash of revolt, the struggles of numerous coups, and multiple occupations and colonization Haiti always found the strength to fight back and remain strong and powerful. A common Haiti proverb reflects the country's resilience and strength:

Ayiti se tè glise; Dèyè mòn, gen mòn which translates to "Haiti is a slippery land; behind the mountains are more mountains."

Haiti and the US connection

Haiti has a strong connection with the US. As already explained, the 1791 revolution (more about this in a subsequent chapter) in Haiti directly impacted US by forcing Napoleon to concede critical French-occupied territories (under the Louisiana Purchase directive) such as Arkansas, Louisiana, Missouri, Nebraska, Oklahoma, Iowa, Minnesota, Kansas, Colorado, the Dakotas, Montana and Wyoming to the US.

This was a time when the US was also fighting for its own independence from European, especially English and French, domination. In 1779, over 500 Haitians took part in the Battle of Savannah. This group of Haitians was referred to as Les Chasseurs Volontaires de Savannah, and in October 2009, a monument was erected in Central Savannah to commemorate the Haitians who fought in this war. After the 1791 revolution in Haiti began, many Haitians settled in Louisiana.

The success of the Haiti Revolt of 1791 was like a ray of hope for many African-Americans in the US whose lives were as miserable as those of Haitian slaves doing backbreaking work for their French colonizers. The flipside of this was that white Americans refused to acknowledge the victory of the Haitian as they feared that such successes could drive the American black slaves to revolt in the US too. If slaves in the US revolted, then the slave-driven economy of the country would be badly affected resulting in the economic downfall for many of the prosperous white Americans. So, like the French, the US also did not acknowledge and accept Haiti's freedom until 1862.

There were many leaders among who exhorted the African-Americans in the US to immigrate to free Haiti to live as free men instead of as slaves in the US. While there were large migration movements to Haiti from the US, a large percentage of these people chose to return to the US driven by language and climactic-related challenges. About 20% of the immigrants chose to make Haiti as their new home. This mass migration forged a strong bond between the US and Haiti.

However, the US occupation of Haiti during the period between 1915 and 1934 soured relationships between the two countries. This US occupation of Haiti added to the instability in the country in the US itself. Moreover, many African-Americans denounced and condemned US' Haiti occupation of a sovereign nation.

A leading African-American who condemned this US occupation of Haiti was James Weldon Johnson, the Executive Secretary of The National Association for the Advancement of Colored People (NAACP). He wrote a series of letters which were published in "The Nation" in which he denounced US' injustice toward Haiti and its people.

In the year 1932, Langston Hughes, a famous poet of those times, traveled to Haiti and met Jacques Roumain, a leading Haitian intellectual. Hughes was highly impressed by Roumain and mentioned his interactions with the man in his autobiographical work titled, "*I Wonder as I Wander: An Autobiographical Journey.*"

Hughes also translated Gouverneurs *de la Rosée,* Roumain's seminal work into English under the title, Masters of the Dew. Therefore, before the modern-day terms like 'transnationalism' and 'cross-border knowledge sharing' were even invented or made popular, such intellectual exchanges were already taking place between Haiti and the US intellectuals.

I take this liberty to dwell on the histories of Haiti and the special connection between France and Haiti to help you understand the deep connection that Creole has to many languages because of the multiple cultures of people that the people of Haiti came in contact with. So, even though history does not have any direct impact on learning the Creole language, this historical cultural connection will help you appreciate the development of various nuances in the language. The next chapter is specifically dedicated to the history of France and Haiti because it is this love-hate relationship that helped in the development of Creole being a language that stands on its own two feet despite being considered a close cousin of the French language.

Chapter 2: Haiti and France

There is a deep love-hate relationship between Haiti and France. Let me start at the very beginning. In about 50 years after Christopher Columbus landed on the island Hispaniola that he himself christened, the local Taino Indians were almost decimated driven by European infections and ruthlessness driving them to hard labor. The Taino Indians were no match for the Spaniards who came thinking there was gold on Hispaniola. Soon, the Spaniards gave up looking for gold in Haiti as they found lots of the yellow metal in Mexico and other American regions.

Then, the French took over. By 1664, the French West Indies Company controlled nearly the whole of Haiti. The French and the Spaniards signed the Treaty of Ryswick wherein France obtained control over all of Haiti and they, in true French spirit, renamed it Saint-Dominique. The French had acres and acres of cocoa, tobacco, indigo, and cotton plantations and there were no more Taino Indians to do their work for them.

So, they kidnapped and brought slaves from Africa to work on these plantations. Driven mercilessness of the French colonizers, these slaves worked so hard on the farms that by the mid 18th century, Saint-Dominique became the wealthiest French colony in the world. Over 75% of the world coffee and more than 40% of Europe's sugar was produced in Haiti or Saint-Dominique. The island came to be known as 'la perle des Antilles," or 'the pearl of Antilles." All this was possible only because of slaves and their unending, backbreaking hard work.

The Haitian Revolution

This was actually an offshoot of the 1789 French Revolution which was promoted by the intellectuals of France such as Montesquieu and Diderot. During the early times of the French Revolution, the concept of liberty, equality and fraternity was limited to France only. While people like Diderot were against slavery, a large percentage of the French bourgeoisie was content to let things lie undisturbed with regard to slavery. After all, wasn't slavery giving them the luxuries and riches that they had become so accustomed to? Hence, they were loath to give up the cheap labor from slavery that would negatively impact their sound financial investments.

Despite this indifference, a small delegation of Black slaves from Saint-Dominique was invited to take part in the National Assembly in Paris to discuss the issue. The Haitian Revolution increased pace and intensity when the white ruling class of Saint-Dominique refused to accept this revolutionary regime that went to Paris. The White land and slave-owners of Saint-Dominique did not want to accept the civic rights bestowed by Paris.

The white landowners revolted against the Léger Felicité Sonthonx, the French Commissioner who visited the island in 1791. He had to counter a fully-fledged rebellion from the White landowners and aristocracy of the island. He had to employ an entire army of Black slaves to defeat this rebellion. The leader of this army of Black slaves was Toussaint Louverture who went on to become one of the greatest generals in the Haiti Revolution.

Toussaint Louverture

It makes sense to spend some time on this great man who opened the way for the freedom of the Black slaves in Haiti and was responsible for the first Slave victory in the world. He was a self-educated remarkable man who defeated the famed Napoleon and got the moniker, "Black Napoleon." With grit and determination, he drove Napoleon out of his beloved country, then called Saint-Dominique.

Although he born a slave, Toussaint learned about Africa from his father who was a free man there before he was kidnapped and brought to Haiti. His father taught him that he was not just a slave but a man with dignity and intelligence. He was lucky to have a master who was kind enough to let him learn to read and write. Toussaint leveraged this advantage to the fullest and read every book he could lay his hands on. He was particularly attracted to the books written by the French Enlightenment philosophers who were highly vocal about individual freedom and rights.

During the 1789 French Revolution, the moderate revolutionaries applied the "Rights of Man" to the free Black men and the mullatos, who were of mixed race. The "Rights of Man" did not fully represent the concept of equality and freedom but it was still something. The plantation owners were unhappy even with this and wanted it retracted. The moderate revolutionaries gave in and retracted the "Rights of Man" in 1791.

The news of this rollback triggered a series of Black revolts in the island of Saint-Dominique and Toussaint become the leader of this widespread revolution. His given name was Toussaint Breda. But, when he became the leader of the slave revolution, he changed his name to Toussaint Louverture. Louverture means 'the one who opens the door."

His people believed that Toussaint was the one who opened the door to their freedom. He led his army of slaves to a brilliant victory and successfully pushed the French army out of their island. Of course, natural reasons such as the French army being attacked by yellow fever helped in the cause of the Haiti Revolution as well. It was as if even Nature wanted to do her best to help the slaves of Haiti attain their independence.

Then after a few more years of instability in France, Napoleon came to power and he ruled like a dictator. He responded favorably to the cries of plantation owners and reinstated slavery in all the French colonies including Haiti. This drove Haiti into a state of war and revolution. By 1803, Napoleon fatigued of the unending revolutions and revolts was ready to sign a peace treaty with Toussaint. In this treaty, Napoleon accepted and recognized that independence of Haiti while Toussaint accepted to retire from public life.

Some months after this treaty was signed, Toussaint was invited to a negotiating meeting where he was promised safe conduct. However, Napoleon retracted on this and on the way to the meeting, Toussaint was captured and held prisoner in the dungeons deep in the mountains. He was killed not by the stroke of a sword but through starvation, neglect and the bitter cold. But his followers continued to fight for freedom and were always a thorn for Napoleon. When he got busy with his European conquests, Napoleon found these far-away possessions difficult to maintain and administer. So, he sold off his possessions of the New World to the US and allowed Haiti to get its freedom and independence from French control.

Louverture and the Black Jacobins

The Black Jacobins were led by Maximilien Robespierre, a vociferous proponent for the abolition of slavery in France. As already mentioned earlier, the French bourgeoisie was more favored to retaining slavery for the sake of a flourishing trade and commerce. Robespierre and his Jacobins fought against this skewed concept of equality by the French bourgeoisie wherein freedom was tending towards freedom of trade rather than individual and civic rights for all.

There followed a Reign of Terror during the time of Robespierre wherein he fanatically fought against the French bourgeoisie's skewed concept of freedom and liberty. During the Reign of Terror, Robespierre had an enormous amount of support from the poor in France and the Black slaves in Haiti. Even to this day, Robespierre is revered by the poor of Haiti.

Hence, the first true concept of equality and liberty and tested and found successful in Haiti. Hence, Haiti should be the center of focus if you want to learn more about the French Revolution too. Moreover, the things that happened during the French and Haitian Revolutions brought the two cultures and people together far closer to each other than before.

Other Haitian revolutionaries

After the deportation and death of Toussaint, General Jacques Dessalines continued to lead the Haitian army towards total independence. In 1803, the Haitian army decimated the French army which was compelled to withdraw when over 50,000 soldiers were killed leading to one of the most triumphant victories for Haiti and its people. In 1804, Haiti was declared a free republic and its constitution was drafted in 1805.

The Haitians had crossed over the racist attitudes of its colonizers and had emerged victorious. Moreover, this first victory for the abolition of slavery became an inspiring precedent for other colored people who were also fighting for independence in different countries. Thus, the Haitians were not just fighters but were ready to lead the world to become a better and more peaceful place wherein culture and prosperity could be shared and enjoyed together.

Present day Haiti

Despite such a glorious history, Haiti continues to struggle against poverty and other economic problems which continue to mar its progress. However, their culture continues to thrive. The language of Creole is something that the Haitians are proud of and they do not hesitate to tell the story of how this language emerged through the tumultuous periods wherein cultures and languages found a landing point in this beautiful nation since the time of Christopher Columbus.

Chapter 3: History of Haitian Creole

One of the official languages of Haiti is Creole. Considering the closeness and the intertwining that has happened between Haiti and France, it comes as no surprise that Creole has a very close connection to French. The seven million population of Haiti and the million Haitians living in foreign lands all speak Creole. Yet, about 10% of the Haitians also speak French which they would have picked up either in school or at home. The Haitians are very proud, and quite rightly so, of their language and even those who speak French believe that Creole gives them a strong sense of national identity.

The Haitians call their native language Kreyol, which, in English, is translated to Creole. In this book, I have used Kreyol and Creole interchangeably; both the words refer to the native language of the Haitians. The English term Creole has its etymological root in a Portuguese word meaning 'raised at home.'

At first, it was used to describe Europeans born and brought up in overseas colonies. Then, the word began to be used for languages that developed in the plantations of European colonies. These plantations usually produced cash crops like coffee, indigo, sugar, and cotton and these farms had slaves brought in from Africa laboring on them.

Haitian Creole is considered to be the most widely spoken as well as the most developed creole languages which were born in the plantations of European colonies that exist today. The plantation colonies that have their own creole language include Guadeloupe, Louisiana, French Guyana, Martinique, and many other island nations on the Indian Ocean. But the largest spoken Creole language in the world is Haitian Creole.

The grammar, vocabulary, and the structure of the Haitian Creole language are all developed well enough to meet all the requirements of its speakers. I just want to reiterate that in this book, when I mention Creole, I am referring to Haitian Creole only.

Formation of Creole

Creole is a result of the efforts of the African slaves to learn the language of their masters when they landed in Haiti (formerly Saint-Dominique). Slaves were brought in from different parts of West Africa and they spoke many languages. If you took even one plantation, you could hear many different African languages being spoken by these slaves kidnapped and brought from various parts of West Africa. Each tribe and culture in Africa speak a different tongue!

Moreover, the French colonizers also spoke different dialects of French. The French spoken by the settlers in Haiti was called Popular and was quite different from the French that was spoken by the ruling class in mainland France. The language spoken by the aristocracy was called Standard French.

The slaves who landed initially also faced a lot of problems communicating with each other and their masters. To improve their communication levels, all the slaves started trying to learn Popular French. The slaves who came in later rarely had direct contact with their French masters and hence did not get to hear so much of Popular French. They only got to hear the French learned by the already existing slaves. This French was a more approximate variety of the original Popular French which was again quite different from the Standard French of the ruling class in France.

Over a period of time, the variety of French that the Haitian slaves spoke became more and more different from the popular French. Soon, the approximate variety became a language by itself and thus the roots of Creole began to grow and flourish. Creole became so popular and individualistic that even the White settlers in the island started learning it and speaking it even within the confines of their home. Thus, all those born and brought up in Haiti, whether Whites or Blacks, began to learn and converse in Creole only.

Yes, almost 90% of Creole has its words borrowed from French and yet many French-speaking people cannot understand Creole. That is the kind of uniqueness Creole developed for itself. There are some reasons as to why Creole and French are fairly different from each other and they are:

- The grammar aspects of the two languages are quite different from each other
- The original words used in Popular French have been replaced with words from Standard French whereas the words taken from Popular French have been retained in Creole
- Some Popular French words underwent changes in meanings too whereas Creole retained the original meanings of the words.

Let me illustrate with an example. The Creole version of "What is your name?" is "Ki jan ou rele?" The French will never understand this because they would say, "Comment vous appelez-vous?" Yet, every word in "Ki jan ou rele?" is French in origin. Here is how it goes:

- Ki is taken from French Qui meaning "what"
- Jan is taken from French genre meaning "manner"
- Ou is taken from French vous meaning "you"
- Heler means to "call"

So, "Ki jan ou rele?" actually translates to "what manner you call (yourself)?" Also, 'heler' which has its roots in Popular French has been replaced with 'appeler' from Standard French. That is where and how the differences between Creole and French lie. But, learning both the languages together is easy as they have common roots and hence this book, "Learn to speak French and Creole." The learning process of the two deeply languages can be a combined one.

The African aspect of Creole

Considering the fact that Creole was developed by and for the slaves from Africa, it is hardly surprising that it has certain aspects of African languages deeply embedded into it. Many experts opine that Creole has its vocabulary from French and grammar from the various African languages spoken by the original slaves. This appears to be a reasonable deduction since African culture is deep-rooted in other aspects of Haitian life such as food, religion and folklore.

Let me give you a couple of examples to show the impact of African languages on Creole. Okra, used a lot of Haitians, is called gumbo, the African name for the vegetable. The popular use of gumbo is carried forward from their African origins. Also, there are a few grammatical occurrences that can be traced back to their African languages. For example, the use of the definite article 'the' in Creole is quite similar to its usage in African languages whereas, in French, the article is placed before the noun. Here is an illustrative example.

- In English, the phrase would read "the house."
- In Standard French, the phrase would read as "la maison."
- In Popular French, the phrase would read as "la maison la." - The second la in Popular French is for emphasis like in English, "that house there."
- In Creole, the phrase would read as "kay la". This is very similar to the grammar of a widely spoken African language, Yoruba, in which this same phrase would be "afe la," ife meaning 'house" in Yoruba.

African languages seemed to have served as filters to the slaves who landed first on Haiti. They heard and picked up words from popular French and combined these words to the grammar of their home language and created phrases and sentences. Aimé Césaire, a famed writer from Martinique, said it beautifully about Creole. He said,

"Creole's body is made from French but its soul is made from African."

Creole has some amount of English and Spanish influence as well depending on which part of the island the speaker lives in or comes from. The spoken language has been in use in 1800s while the first Creole dictionary was created in the year 1979.

The future of Creole

The fact that I have chosen to write a book on this wonderful language should tell you my personal beliefs on the future of this language. Today, Creole is recognized as an official language of Haiti along with French. It has its own spelling today. Although all the government official documents are maintained in French, Creole is increasingly being used in media and in the education field. The future citizens of Haiti are being trained and educated to take the legacy of the language forward into the next generations.

The fact that Creole is now a fully functional and recognized official language of Haiti empowers those people who know only Creole to participate actively in nation building by standing for elections and being involved in public forums without fear of not being understood. Creole-speaking people can actively involve themselves in the economic, political, and cultural progress of their country.

Chapter 4: Alphabets in Creole and French

The set of alphabets is a great place to start learning a language. So, here goes the set of alphabets for Creole:

- A – *ah* – pronounced by opening your mouth and saying ah
- B – beh – pronounced as in "San Francisco Bay" and cutting it short
- C – seh – pronounced as in "say" and again, cutting it short
- D – deh – as in 'day' but cut short
- E – eh – pronounced like the English "A" (rhyming with 'say') and cutting it short
- F – eff – pronounced the same as the English "F"
- G – jeh – pronounced like the 'g' in the word "collage"
- H – osh – said like the way you say Osh in Osh Kosh
- I – ee – said like in "eel" or "eat"
- J – jee – here, the j in "jee" should also be said like the 'g' in 'collage'
- K – kaw – said like how you would say the word 'cop' but without the p
- L – el – pronounced the same as the English "L"
- M – em - pronounced the same as the English "M"
- N – en – pronounced like the English N
- O – oh – said like the English 'o' but cutting it a bit short
- P – peh – pronounced like "pay the bills" but again cutting it a bit short
- Q – kee – pronounced like key in 'lock and key'
- R – eya – said like how a horseman would say to goad his horse
- S – es – said the same way as English S
- T – the – pronounced as 'tape' but without the p and cutting it short
- U – gwo ee – pronounced exactly like how I have written the word

- V – veh
- W – doob leh veh
- X – eeks – like the English colloquial for shouting out in fear or disgust
- Y – ee greg
- Z – zed

Here are some commonly used alphabet pairs and how they need to be pronounced:

Ou – oo

Example: *tout moun* – Tout is said like "toot" in "toot the horn" and "moun" is said like "moon" in "new moon." Tout means "every or all" and moun means "people or person." So, "tout moun" means all people or everyone.

Ay – said like I in I love you

Example: *lay* – pronounced like "lie" in "One must not tell a lie" and the word means garlic. *Kay* – said like "kai" and the word means house.

Ey – pronounced like a word that rhymes with play

Example: Fey – said like how you would call Fay, a girl's name in English and Fey in Creole means sheet (as in sheet of paper) or leaf.

é and ò

The words é and ò are pronounced slightly differently from the usual e and o and the best way to learn how to say this is to use hear it from a Creole-speaking person.

Nasal sounds that do not exist in English - For nasal sounds, the 'n' syllable is not really pronounced.

For example, 'an' is pronounced 'uh' with a nasal twang. 'Blan' means white. 'Tan' means time or weather. 'Pan' is for peacock. 'Pran' means take. 'San' means blood or without

'en' is pronounced as 'eh' with a nasal sound. 'chen' means dog, 'swen' means care, 'pen' means bread, 'nen' means nose.

'on' is said like 'oh' with a nasal sound. 'son' means sound, 'bon' means good, 'tonton' means uncle, 'fason' means manner or way, 'balon' means ball, 'gason' means man.

If you should actually pronounce the 'n' sound after a, e, or o, then the spelling will have two 'ns' in it; for example, fonn is pronounced with the sound of the 'n' and means melt. Similarly, 'balenn' means candle, 'tann' means wait, 'kann' means sugar cane, 'chenn' means chain or necklace, 'sispann' means to stop, 'renn' means queen, 'ponn' means (to lay) eggs, 'grenn' means seed or bead or a unit.

Some more examples of letter combinations and their pronunciations

Ch – is pronounced like 'sh' in English. For example, 'chay' would be said like ch=sh and ay=I and hence 'chay' would be said as 'shy' and it means load. 'Chita' means to sit down, 'chapo' means hat, 'chini' means caterpillar, 'chou' (pronounced like shoe) means cabbage.

J – is pronounced like the 'g' in the English word 'collage.' Dj sounds like the English 'J.' 'Djab' is said like the word, job, in English and it means demon.

Q – is not used in pure Creole though some Frenchified versions use it and it pronounced as 'kee'

C – is never used by itself but only in combination with 'h' to form 'ch' which has the sound of 'sh' in English

U or x – is also not used in true Creole

R - I have to spend some time on the letter 'r.' This is similar to French 'r' but still is different. To many, it might sound like a 'w.' To pronounce 'r' in Creole, say the sound English 'r' without closing your mouth in any manner.

Other letters sound just like the English alphabet. Letter combinations like sh, gh, th, ph, etc do not exist in Creole.

Set of French alphabets and their pronunciations

http://bit.ly/2rYvcCp
https://www.youtube.com/watch?v=te7mciqgPv4

French alphabets also contain the same 26 alphabets as in English though the pronunciations are different and depend on accent marks and letter combinations. So, here is the list of French alphabets:

- A – ah
- B – beh
- C – seh
- D – deh
- E – uh
- F – eff
- G – zheh (like the English 'g' sound in the word 'collage')
- H – ahsh
- I – ee
- J – zhee
- K – kah
- L – ell
- M – em
- N – en
- O – oh
- P – peh
- Q – koo

- R – air
- S – ess
- T – teh
- U – ooh
- V – veh
- W – doobl-veh
- X – eeks
- Y – ee-grek
- Z – zed

French accents – Accent is what makes French unique and hence it makes sense to spend some time on the different accents and how they are denoted in the written language. The accents denote the sounds that need to be used by speaking the words. Moreover, each accent mark is unique to the letter. The different French accents include:

- Acute accent – é – as in éléphant: elephant
- Grave accent – à, ò, and ù – là; there, où; where, fièvre; fever
- Circumflex accent – â, ê, î, ô, û – être; to be, gateau, chômage; unemployment
- Trema – ë, ï, ü, ÿ – maïs; corn, Noël; Christmas,
- Cidella – Ç only – FRANÇAIS – French

So, the letters for Creole and French are quite similar and the differences lie in the grammar and the way they are pronounced. Accents play a huge role in making the difference between the two related languages easily discernible even to the novice learner. The next chapter talks about numbers in both the languages.

Chapter 5: Cardinal and Ordinal Numbers in French and Creole

Numbers are an essential element of communication and conversation. This chapter deals with both cardinal and ordinal numbers in Creole and French.

Cardinal Numbers in Creole

https://www.youtube.com/watch?v=t9LnbhwDAjs
http://bit.ly/2sdys14

- Zero - Zewo
- One – en or youn
- Two – de
- Three – twa
- Four – kat
- Five – senk
- Six – sis
- Seven – sèt
- Eight – uit
- Nine – nèf
- Ten – dis
- Eleven – onz
- Twelve – douz
- Thirteen – trèz
- Fourteen – katòz
- Fifteen – kenz
- Sixteen – sèz
- Seventeen – disèt (dis or 10 + set or 7)
- Eighteen – dizwit (dis or 10 + uit or 8)
- Nineteen – diznèf (dis or 10 + nèf or 9)
- Twenty – ven

En or Youn

Before I move on to the next numbers, let me give you a small note on the use of 'en, youn' or one. En has to be used only to refer to numerical identifications like phone numbers, pin numbers, numbered lists, IDs, etc. Here are some examples of when to use en and when to use youn.

Phone numbers – 'My phone number begins with one' will read as Nimewo mwen kòmanse ak **en**

Identification codes, pins, and numbers – 'My ID number starts with one' will read as ID mwen kòmanse ak **en**

Numbered lists – 'The number one on the list' will read as 'Nimewo **en** nan lis la'

During all other times, you will use youn (which is also called yon or yonn). For example, 'I have a car' will read as Mwen gen **yon** machin. 'You have an orange' will be Ou gen **yon** zoranj

Numbers 10-100

- Ten – dis
- Twenty – ven
- Thirty – trant
- Forty – karant
- Fifty – senkant
- Sixty – swasant
- Seventy – swasanndis (60 + 10)
- Eighty – katreven
- Ninety – katrevendis (70 + 10)
- Hundred – san

So, you can use these for giving approximations. For example, suppose someone asked you, Kon byen?" which is "How many?" in

Creole, you can say, 'anviwon ven' which means 'around 20' instead of specifically saying '23' or 'venntwa.'

Numbers 20 to 69

Numbers 21, 31, 41, and 51 will have the previous ten as the prefix and end in 'eyen' which literally translates to 'and-one' in English.

Let us take *21-30* first and then we will move to the next ten numbers: 21 – venteyen, 22 – vennde, 23 – venntwa, 24 – vennkat, 25 – vennsenk, 26 – vennsis, 27 – vennsèt, 28 – ventuit, 29 – ventnèf, 30 – trant.

Similarly, *31-40* will be as follows: 31 – tranteyen, 32 – trannde, 33 – tranntwa, 34 – trannkat, 35 – trannsenk, 36 – trannsis, 37 – trannsèt, 38 – trantuit, 39 – trantnèf, 40 – karant.

41-50 will be as follows: 41 – karanteyen, 42 – karannde, 43 – karanntwa, 44 – karannkat, 45 – karannsenk, 46 – karannsis, 47 – karannsèt, 48 – karantuit, 49 – karantnèf, 50 – senkant

51-59 will be as follows: 51 - senkanteyen, 52 – senkannde, 53 – senkanntwa, 54 – senkannkat, 55 – senkannsek, 56 – senkannsis, 57 – senkannsèt, 58 – senkantuit, 59 – senkantnèf, 60 – swasant

61-69 will go as follows: 61 – swasanteyen, 62 – swasannde, 63 – swasanntwa, 64 – swasannkat, 65 – swasannsenk, 66 – swasannsis, 67 – swasannsèt, 68 – swasantuit, 69 – swasantnèf

Numbers 70 to 100

For 70 in Creole, you must add 60 (swasant) to 10 (dis) and you get swasanndis. For 71, you add 60 (swasant) to 11 (onz) and you get swasann-onz, for 72, you add 60 to 12 (douz) to get swasanndouz, and so on.

70-80 will be as follows: 70 – swasanndis, 71 – swasann-onz, 72 – swasann-douz, 73 – swasann-trez, 74 – swasann-katòz, 75 – swasann-kenz, 76 – swasann-sèz, 77 – swasann-disèt, 78 – swasann-dizuit, 79 – swasann-diznèf, 80 – katreven

81 – 90 will be as follows: 81 – katrevenen, 82 – katrevende, 83 – katreventwa, 84 – katrevenkat, 85 – katrevensenk, 86, katrevensis, 87 – katrevensèt, 88 – katrevenuit, 89 – katreven-nèf, 90 – katrevendis (80+10)

91 – 100 will be as follows: 91 (80 + 11) – katreven-onz, 92 – katreven-douz, 93 – katreven-trez, 94 - katreven-katòz, 95 – katreven-kenz, 96 – katreven-sèz, 97 – katreven-disèt. 98 – katreven-dizuit, 99 – katreven-diznèf, 100 – san

Knowing the pattern for counting is the key element in mastering numbers in Creole. It might appear complicated initially, but once you get the basic pattern right, you will be able to count easily in Creole.

I would like to add the following numbers to the list: 100 – san, 1,000 – mil, 1,000,000 - milyon

Ordinal numbers in Creole

Here are the ordinal numbers in Creole:

- First – premye
- Second – dezyèm
- Third – twazyèm
- Fourth – katrizyèm
- Fifth – senkyèm
- Sixth – sizyèm
- Seventh – setyèm
- Eighth – uityèm
- Ninth – nevyèm

- Tenth – dizyèm
- Eleventh – onzyèm
- Twelfth – douzyèm
- Thirteenth – trèzyèm
- Fourteenth – katòrzyèm
- Fifteenth – kenzyèm
- Sixteenth – sèzyèm
- Seventeenth – setyèm
- Eighteenth – wityèm
- Nineteenth – diznevyèm
- Twentieth – ventyèm
- Once – yon fwa
- Twice – de fwa

Cardinal Numbers in French (the phrases in the [box] brackets refer to the pronunciation

- Zero – zèro – [Zay-ro]
- One – un – [uh with a nasal sound]
- Two – deux – [duhr]
- Three – trois – [twa]
- Four – quatre – [katr]
- Five – cinq – [sank]
- Six – six – [sees]
- Seven – sept – [set]
- Eight – huit – [weet]
- Nine – neuf – [nurf]
- Ten – dix – [dees]
- Eleven – onze – [onz]
- Twelve – douze – [dooz]
- Thirteen – trèize – [trez]
- Fourteen – quatorze – [katorz]
- Fifteen – quinze – [kanz]
- Sixteen – seize – [sez]
- Seventeen – dix-sept – [dees-set] (dis or 10 + set or 7)

- Eighteen – dix – huit – [dees-weet] (dis or 10 + uit or 8)
- Nineteen – dix-neuf – [dees-nurf] (dis or 10 + nèf or 9)
- Twenty – vingt – [van]

Numbers 10-100

- Ten – dix – [dees]
- Twenty – vingt – [van]
- Thirty – trente – [tront]
- Forty – quarante – [karont]
- Fifty – cinqante – [sank-ont]
- Sixty – soixante -]swan-sont]
- Seventy – soixante-dix – [swa-sont-dees] (60 + 10)
- Eighty – quatre-vingts – [katravan]
- Ninety – quatre-vingt-dix – [katravendees] (80 + 10)
- Hundred – cent – [son]

Numbers 20 to 69

Numbers 21, 31, 41, and 51 will have the previous ten as the prefix and end in et-un, pronounced as 'ey-uh' which literally translates to 'and-one' in English.

Let us take *21-30* first and then we will move to the next ten numbers: 21 – vingt et un, 22 – vingt-deux, 23 – vingt-trois, 24 – vingt-quatre, 25 – vingt-cinq, 26 – vingt-six, 27 – vingt-sept, 28 – vingt-huit, 29 – vingt-neuf, 30 – trente.

Similarly, *31-40* will be as follows: 31 – Trente et un, 32 – Trente-deux, 33 – Trente-trois, 34 – Trente-quatre, 35 – Trente-cinq, 36 – Trente-six,37 – Trente-sept, 38 – Trente-huit, 39 – Trente-neuf, 40 – quarante.

41-50 will be as follows: 41 – quarante et un, 42 – quarante-deux, 43 – quarante-trois, 44 – quarante-quatre, 45 – quarante-cinq, 46 – quarante-six, 47 – quarante-sept, 48 – quarante-huit, 49 – quarante-neuf, 50 – cinquante.

51-59 will be as follows: 51 - cinquante et un, 52 – cinquante-deux, 53 – cinquante-trois, 54 – cinquante-quatre, 55 – cinquante-cinq, 56 – cinquante-six, 57 – cinquante-sept, 58 – cinquante-huit, 59 – cinquante-neuf, 60 – soixante.

61-69 will go as follows: 61 – soixante et un, 62 – soixante-deux, 63 – soixante-trois, 64 – soixante-quatre, 65 – soixante-cinq, 66 – soixante-six, 67 – soixante-sept, 68 – soixante-huit, 69 – soixante-neuf.

Numbers 70 to 100

In French too, for 70 (just like in Creole), you must add 60 (soixante) to 10 (dix) and you get soixante-dix –swa-sont-dees]. For 71, you add 60 (soixante) to 11 (onze) and you get soixante-et-onze [swa-sont-ay-onz], for 72, you add 60 to 12 (douze) to get soixante-douze [swa-sont-dooz], and so on.

70-80 will be as follows: 70 – soixante-dix, 71 – soixante-et-onze, 72 – soixante-douze, 73 – soixante-treize, 74 – soixante-quatorze, 75 – soixante-quinze, 76 – soixante-seize, 77 – soixante-dix-sept, 78 – soixante-dix-huit, 79 – soixante-dix-neuf, 80 – quatre-vingts

81 – 90 will be as follows: 81 – quatre-vingt-un, 82 – quatre-vingt-deux, 83 – quatre-vingt-trois, 84 – quatre-vingt-quatre, 85 – quatre-vingt-cinq, 86, quatre-vingt-six 87 – quatre-vingt-sept, 88 – quatre-vingt-huit, 89 – quatre-vingt-neuf, 90 – quatre-vingt-dix (80+10)

91 – 100 will be as follows: 91 (80 + 11) – quatre-vingt-onze, 92 – quatre-vingt-douze, 93 – quatre-vingt-treize, 94 - quatre-vingt-quatorze, 95 – quatre-vingt-quinze, 96 – quatre-vingt-seize, 97 – quatre-vingt-dix-sept. 98 – quatre-vingt-dix-huit, 99 – quatre-vingt-dix-neuf, 100 – cent

Ordinal numbers in French

Here are the ordinal numbers in French:

- First – premier
- Second – deuxième
- Third – troisième
- Fourth – quatrième
- Fifth – cinquième
- Sixth – sixième
- Seventh – septième
- Eighth – huitième
- Ninth – neuvième
- Tenth – dixième
- Eleventh – onzième
- Twelfth – douzième
- Thirteenth – treizième
- Fourteenth – quatorzième
- Fifteenth - quinzième
- Sixteenth – seizième
- Seventeenth – dix-septième
- Eighteenth – dix-huitième
- Nineteenth – dix-neuvième
- Twentieth – vingtième
- Once – une- fois-que – [ou-fwa-ke]
- Twice – dois fwa – [de fwa]

A clear difference that I can see between Creole and French is the fact that Creole is spelled more like the same way it is pronounced whereas French has accents which have to be learned and mastered before you can read and say the words perfectly.

Chapter 6: Months of the Year, Days of the Week, and Time

MONTHS OF THE YEAR IN CREOLE

- January – janvye
- February – fevriye
- March – mas
- April - avril
- May – me
- June – jen
- July – jiyè
- August - out
- September – septanm
- October – oktòb
- November – novanm
- December – desanm

MONTHS OF THE YEAR IN FRENCH

- January – janvier – [zhah(n)-vyay]
- February – février – [fay-vree-yay]
- March – mars – [mahrs]
- April - avril – [ah-vreel]
- May – mai – [meh]
- June – juin – [zhwa(n)]
- July – juillet – [zhwee-eh]
- August - août – [oo *or* oot]
- September – septembre – [sehp-tah(n)br]
- October – octobre – [ohk-tohbr]
- November – novembre – [noh-vah(n)br]
- December – décembre – [day-sah(n)br]

The month names are quite similar to their English versions and hence can be easy of you to learn. Remember that in Creole and in French, month names are not capitalized except when they are the first word in a sentence. To say 'in January," you would say, 'en Janvier."

DAYS OF THE WEEK IN CREOLE

- Monday - lendi
- Tuesday – madi
- Wednesday – mekredi
- Thursday – jedi
- Friday – vandredi
- Saturday – samdi
- Sunday – dimanch

DAYS OF THE WEEK IN FRENCH

- Monday - lundi
- Tuesday – mardi
- Wednesday – mercredi
- Thursday – jeudi
- Friday – vendredi
- Saturday – samedi
- Sunday - dimanche

Days of the week are also not capitalized in French and in Creole except when at the beginning of a new sentence.

TELLING TIME IN CREOLE

Now, that you know your numbers quite well, you can use that to tell time as well. Here are some words used for telling time in Creole.

- Hour - lè, è
- Number of hours - èdtan
- Minute – minit
- Second (time) - segond
- o'clock – è
- morning - maten
- Afternoon - apre midi

- Day - jounen, jou
- Night - aswè, swa
- Noon – midi
- Midnight – minwi
- Early - bonè
- Late – anreta
- On time – alè
- Quarter past an hour – enka
- Half past an hour - e demi or edmi
- 45 minutes past an hour – twaka
- 45 minutes to an hour – mwenka

How to tell time in Creole

Time in Creole is said as follows: Number of the hour followed by è. Here are all the hours:

- Inè, - one o'clock
- Dezè – two o'clock
- Twazè – three o'clock
- Katrè – four o'clock
- Senkè – five o'clock
- Sizè – six o'clock
- Setè – seven o'clock
- Uitè – eight o'clock
- Nevè – nine o'clock
- Dizè – ten o'clock
- Onzè – eleven o'clock
- Midi for noon and Munui for midnight (already mentioned above as well)

Here are some common phrases used for time-related conversations:

What time is it? - Ki lè li ye?

If you want to know the time of an event of when it is going to take place, then simply say 'Ki lè' followed by the description of the event. For example, if you want to ask 'when is the meeting?' you would say, 'Ki lè reyinyon an?' The 'reyinyon' or the meeting or the event will follow the phrase 'Ki lè.'

- When is the interview? - Ki lè entèvyou a?
- When is the assembly? - Ki lè asanble a?
- When is the meeting? - Ki lè reyinyon an?

The words 'a' and 'an' are definite articles which in Creole come after the noun (explained in one of the earlier chapters). Examples of how say the hour:

- It is five o'clock - Li senkè
- It is six o'clock - Li sizè
- It is seven o'clock - Li setè
- It is eleven o'clock - Li onzè

To say the time with minutes, simply say the hour as above and then the number of minutes following that. Here are some examples:

- It is five ten (5:10) – Li senkè dis
- It is six twenty (6:20) – Li sizè ven
- It is seven thirty (7:30) – Li setè trant
- It is quarter past five (5:15) - Li senkè enka
- It is half past five (5:30) - Li senkè edmi
- It is quarter to six (5:45) - Li sizè mwennka

TELLING TIME IN FRENCH

To tell time in the French language, you will say il est followed by the hour (number) followed by heure (hour in French). For example, 'it is two o'clock' will be 'il est deux heures.' Only for one o'clock, you will use heure; for everything else, it will be heures. So, it is one o'clock will be il est une heure. Please note that you have to use the feminine version instead of the masculine un because heure is feminine.

In English where the o'clock can be missed while telling time. For example, you can simply say, it is five to mean it is five o'clock. However, in French, the heure should not be missed at all. The 'il est' is commonly left out by people quite familiar with the language but not the heure. For example: What time is it? - quelle heure est-il? You can say eight o'clock which would be huit heures.

Using minutes to tell time in French

Using minutes while telling time in French has a few twists and turns. So, let us focus on it in this section. There are separate ways to say the first 30 minutes and the next minutes of the hour.

For one to thirty minutes past an hour (1 to 30), you will have to simply add the number of minutes after the mentioned hour. Examples are as under:

- It is 2:10 – il est deux heures dix (In a literal sense, the French way of saying is two hours ten)
- It is 7:25 – il est sept heures vingt-cinq (Seven hours twenty five)

There are some special words for quarter past, half past, and quarter to as in Creole (after all, French is the mother of Creole). They are as follows:

For quarter past the hour, you will say et quart (which literally means 'and a quarter'). Here is an example: Quarter past one (or 1:15) would be 'il est une heure et quart.'

For half past the hour, you will say et demie (which literally means 'and a half'). Here is an example: Half past one (or 1:30) would be 'il est une heure et demie.'

For the next thirty past the hour (31-59), you must say the next hour followed by moins (which is 'minus' in French) the number of minutes. Here are some examples:

- For three fifty (3:50) – il est quartre heures moins dix (this literally translates to ten minutes less than or minus four o'clock)
- For seven forty (7:40) ' il est huit heures moins vingt (literally meaning 20 minutes less than or minus eight o'clock)

For quarter to an hour (as in 8:45 which is quarter to nine in English, you will say, moins le quart (which is literally minus the quarter). For example, 2:45 or quarter to three will be 'il est trois heures moins le quart).

French also has specific words for noon and midnight which are 'midi' and 'minuit' respectively. It is important to remember not to use these two words with the word 'heures.' Let us see an example: If you want to say 'it is midnight' in French, you will simply say, 'il est minuit.'

Some more important time related words in French:

- Morning – le matin; '6:30 AM' will be 'six heures et demie du matin.'
- Afternoon – l'après-midi; '5 PM will be 'cinq heures de l'après-midi'
- Night or evening – du soir; '7 PM' will be 'sept heures du soir'

So, this is the months of the year, days of the week, and time-related words and phrases in Creole and French. The next two chapters deal with useful words, phrases, and sentences.

Chapter 7: Useful Words and Phrases

Popularly used fruits and vegetables in French and Creole

- **English – French – Creole**
- Apple – pomme – pòm
- Bananas – banane – fig
- Potatoes - pomme de terre – pòmdetè
- Tomatoes – tomate – tomat
- Onions – oignon – zonyon
- Beetroot - betterave rouge - betterave rouge
- Carrot – carotte - karòt
- Cucumber – concombre - konkonb
- Garlic – ail – lay
- Lemon – citron - sitron
- Corn/maize – maïs - mayi
- Pear – poire – pwa
- Orange – orange - oranj
- Pineapple – ananas - anana
- Strawberry – fraise - frèz

Commonly used colors in French and Creole

- **English – French – Creole**
- Red – rouge – wouj
- Blue – bleu – ble
- Black – noir – nwa
- Green – vert – vèt
- Purple – violet – violet
- Grey – grise – gri
- White – blanc – blan
- Pink – rose – ròz
- Brown – marron – maron
- Yellow – jaune - jon

Some food items and food-related words in French and Creole

- **English – French – Creole**
- Breakfast – déjeuner - manje maten
- Lunch - le déjeuner - manje midi
- Dinner - le dîner – dine
- Milk – Lait – lèt
- Coffee – café – kafe
- Bread – pain - pèn

Words associated with relatives and family

- **English – French – Creole**
- Boy – garçon – gason
- Girl – fille – fi
- Son – fils – gason
- Daughter – fille – fi
- Brother – frère – frè
- Sister – sœur – sè
- Man – homme – gason
- Woman – femme – fanm
- Father – père – papa
- Mother – mère – manman
- Grandfather - grand-père - gran pè
- Grandmother - grand-mère – grann
- Uncle – oncle – tonton
- Aunt – tante - matant

Terms for weather and related sensations

- **English – French – Creole**
- Sunny - ensoleillé - li fè soley
- Windy - venté – van
- Rainy - pluvieux - lapli ap tombe
- Snowy - neigeux - la nèj ap tombe
- Cold – froid – frèt
- Hot - chaud - cho

House locations

- **English – French – Creole**
- Toilet - toilette – twalèt
- Room - chambre – chanm
- Kitchen – cuisine – kwizin
- Table – table – tablo
- Bedroom - chambre – chanm

Some commonly used greetings in Creole

- Welcome – Byen venu, V V byenvini, N bèlantre
- Hello - Bonjou
- How are you? - Sak pase? Koman ou ye? Ki jan ou ye?
- Responses to 'How are you?' - Mwen byen (I'm well), N'ap boule, M ap boule (I'm fine, lit. 'I'm on fire'), Kon si, kon sa (So, so), M ap viv (I'm living), et ou (mem)? (and you?)
- Long time no see - Sa fè lontan, Sa fe lon temps nou pa we
- What is your name? - Koman ou rele?, Ki jan ou rele?, Ki non ou?, Ki non w?
- My name is… - M rele ..., Mwen rele..., Non m se...
- Where are you from? - Ki kote ou sòti?, Kote ou sòti?
- I am from… - M'soti...
- Pleased to meet you – Anchante, M'kontan fè konesans ou, Mwe kontan fe konesana ou, Se youn plaisir fè konesans ou
- Good morning – Bon maten (you can use Bonjou anytime of the day but Bon maten specifically is for "good morning")
- Good evening – Bonswa
- Good night – Bonn nui, Bonswa, Bonswa et bon rev
- Goodbye (parting phrases) – Adye, Orevwa, Babay, N a wè pi ta, A pi ta (*see you later*),
A demen (*until tomorrow*)
- Good luck – Bon chans
- Cheers or Good Health (greetings while toasting) - Ochan! Sante! Onè Respè!
- Have a nice day - Pase yon bònn jounen, Bònn jounen
- Have a good meal (or Bon appétit) – Bon apeti

- Have a nice journey (Bon voyage) - Bon vwayaj
- Do you understand? – Ou konprann? Eske ou konprann?
- I understand – Mwen konprann
- I do not understand - Mwen pa komprann
- Yes – Wi
- No – non
- Maybe – Petèt
- I do not know - Mwen pa konnen
- Please talk more slowly (or can you please talk more slowly) - Souple pale dousma, Ou ka pale dousman souple?
- Please say again - Ou ka repete souple?
- Please write it down - Es'ke ou ka ecri'l, tanpri?
- Do you talk English? – Eske ou pale angle?
- Do you talk Creole? - Eske ou pale kreyòl?
- Yes, a little… (response to do you talk English or Creole?) - Wi, piti piti, Wi, on ti kal
- How do you say (here you can fill up what you want to be translated)… in Creole? - Kijan ou di ... an kreyòl? Kij an yo di...an kreyòl?, Kòman ou di ... an Kreyòl??
- Excuse me – Eskize mwen, Eskize m
- How much is this? – Konbyen?
- Sorry (for apology or asking for pardon) – Dezole, Mwen regret sa, Padon
- Please – souple
- Thank you – Mesi, Mesi ampil
- Response to thank you – Merite, Padekwa, De ryen
- Where is the toilet? - Kote twalèt la?
- Will you dance with me? - Eske ou vle danse?
- I love you - Mwen renmen w
- I miss you - Mwen sonje w
- Get well soon - Fè mye tale
- Leave me alone! - Ki te'm anrepo'm!
- Go away! - Ale vou zan!
- Fire! – Dife!

- Help! – Anmwe
- Stop – Rete
- Call the police - Rele la polis!
- Christmas and New Year Greetings - Jwaye Nowèl e Bònn Ane
- Birthday greetings - Bonn fèt, Erez anivèsè
- Easter greetings - Bònn fèt pak

Some commonly used words and phrases in French

- Welcome – bienvenu, accueillir
- Hello - Bonjour, allo
- How are you? - comment allez-vous
- Responses to 'How are you?' - je vais bien
- Long time no see - ça fait longtemps
- What is your name? - quel est votre nom, comment t'appelles-tu
- My name is… - mon nom est
- Where are you from? - d'où êtes-vous
- I am from… - Je veins de
- Pleased to meet you – heureux de vous rencontrer
- Good morning – bon matin
- Good evening – bonsoir
- Good night – bonne nuit
- Goodbye (parting phrases) – au revoir, en revoir, jusqu'à demain (until tomorrow)
- Good luck – bonne chance, bon vent
- Cheers or Good Health (greetings while toasting) - Santé, à votre santé
- Have a nice day – bonne journèe
- Have a good meal (or Bon appétit) – bon appétit
- Have a nice journey (Bon voyage) - fais bon voyage
- Do you understand? – Comprenez-vous?
- I understand – je comprends
- I do not understand - Je ne comprends pas
- Yes – Oui
- No – No, aucun

- Maybe – peut être
- I do not know - je ne sais pas
- Please talk more slowly (or can you please talk more slowly) - Parlez plus lentement
- Please say again - Dites-le à nouveau
- Please write it down - s'il vous plaît écrivez-le
- Do you talk English? – parlez vous anglais
- Do you talk French? - parlez-vous français
- Yes, a little… (response to do you talk English or French?) - Oui un peu
- Excuse me – excusez-moi
- How much is this? – combien ça coûte
- Sorry (for apology or asking for pardon) – désolé, moche, piteux
- Please – plaire, plaise, plait
- Thank you – merci
- Response to thank you – vous êtes les bienvenus (you are welcome)
- Where is the toilet? - Où sont les toilettes
- Will you dance with me? - danseras-tu avec moi
- I love you - je te aime
- I miss you - tu me manque
- Get well soon - guérissez bientôt
- Leave me alone! - laissez-moi seule
- Go away! - allez-vous en
- Stop – cesser
- Call the police - appelle la police
- Christmas greetings - Salutations de Noël
- New year greetings - salutations de nouvelle année
- Birthday greetings - souhaits d'anniversaire
- Easter greetings - Salutations de pâques

Again, it would seem that the words and phrases in French and Creole are quite similar and the differences lie only in the accent and the grammar.

Chapter 8: Some More Useful Phrases

Some more useful phrases in French

- 'à cause de' - because of, due to – this is used normally when you want to blame someone or something
- 'à la fois' - at the same time – Used as a synonym for simultaneously
- 'ah bon (?)' - oh really? I see - Used normally as an interjection during a conversation
- 'à la limite'- at most, in a pinch
- 'à la française'- in the French style or manner – Used in relation to France and the French
- 'à la rigueur' - or even, if need be - used when you are unsure about the exact measure or count
- à la vôtre !- cheers! – used for toasting purposes
- à la une - front page news
- allons-y! - let's go!
- à peine - hardly
- à mon avis - in my opinion
- a priori - at first glance, in principle
- à peu près - about, approximately, nearly
- au cas où - just in case
- à tes souhaits - bless you
- au contraire - on the contrary
- au fur et à mesure - as, while
- au fait- by the way
- avoir l'air (de) - to look (like)
- au lieu de - instead of, rather than
- bien dans sa peau - content, comfortable, at ease with oneself
- bien entendu - of course, obviously
- bien sûr - of course
- blague à part - seriously, all kidding aside
- ça alors - how about that, my goodness

- ça marche - ok, that works
- ça m'est égal - it's all the same to me
- ça ne fait rien - never mind, it doesn't matter
- ça va (?) - how's it going?, I'm fine
- ça vaut le coup - it's worth it
- c'est - it is
- d'ailleurs - moreover, might I add
- déjà vu - already seen
- de trop - too much / many
- du tout - not/none at all
- dis donc / dites donc - wow, by the way
- du coup - as a result
- du jour au lendemain - overnighten effet - indeed, that's right
- en fait - in fact
- enfin - well, I mean
- en retard – late
- et j'en passé - and that's not all
- et patati et patata - and so on and so forth
- entendre dire que - to hear that
- entendre parler de - to hear about something being talked about by someone
- entre chien et loup   at dusk, twilight
- est-ce que – this phrase allows you to turn statements into questions
- et j'en passe   and that's not allfais gaffe - watch out, be careful
- fais voir - let me see
- faire cadeau - to give or to let off easily
- faire le pont - to make it a long weekend
- figure-toi - guess what, get this
- 'fin - well, I mean
- grâce à - thanks to
- il est - it is (we have seen many examples of this especially in the 'telling time' chapter)
- il faut – it is necessary

- il y a - there is, there are
- il y a quelque chose qui cloche – something is amiss or wrong
- Je n'en reviens pas - I can't believe it
- Je n'y peux rien - There's nothing I can do about it
- J'arrive! - I'm on my way!
- ma foi - frankly, indeed, well
- métro, boulot – the rat race
- n'est-ce pas? - Right? Isn't that so?
- on ne sait jamais - you never know
- On y va? - Shall we go? Ready?
- par contre - whereas, on the other hand
- pas de probleme - no problem
- par exemple - for example, such as; oh my, well really!
- pas mal - not bad, quite a bit
- pas du tout - not at all
- plus ça change... - the more things change...
- pas terrible - not that great, nothing special
- prendre une decision - to make a decision
- revenons à nos moutons – let us revert to the subject at hand
- rien à voir – have nothing to do with
- sans blague – seriously or leaving all kidding/jokes aside
- si ce n'est pas indiscret - if it is not too personal a question
- si tu veux - if you will

Some more useful phrases in Creole

- because of, due to – paske nan
- at the same time - an menm tan an
- 'oh really? I see - oh reyèlman! mwen wè
- at most, in a pinch - nan pifò
- or even, if need be - si yo bezwen
- front page news - devan paj nouvèl
- let's go! - kite yo ale
- hardly - a pèn
- in my opinion - nan opinyon mwen

- at first glance, in principle - nan prensip
- about, approximately, nearly - apeprè
- just in case - jis nan ka
- bless you - beni ou
- on the contrary - sou kontrè a
- by the way - nan chemen an
- to look (like) - yo gade tankou
- instead of, rather than - olye pou yo
- content, comfortable, at ease with oneself - nan fasilite ak tèt li
- of course, obviously - nan kou
- seriously, all kidding aside - oserye, blag apa
- my goodness - bonte m'
- ok, that works - ok, ki travay
- it's all the same to me - li nan tout menm bagay la tou m'
- never mind, it doesn't matter - pa janm tèt ou, li pa gen pwoblèm
- it's worth it - li la vo li
- it is - li se
- moreover, might I add - Anplis
- already seen - deja wè
- too much / many - twòp bagay
- not/none at all - pa nan tout
- indeed, that's right - tout bon, ki bon
- in fact - an reyalite
- well, I mean - byen, mwen vle di
- late - an reta
- and that's not all - e ke sa a se pa tout
- and so on and so forth - ak sou sa ak pou fè
- watch out, be careful - gade soti, dwe fè atansyon
- let me see - ban mwen wè
- I can't believe it - Mwen pa ka kwè ke li
- There's nothing I can do about it - Pa gen anyen mwen kapab fè sou li
- I'm on my way! - Mwen se sou wout mwen!
- the rat race - ras la rat

- Right? Isn't that so? - Dwa? Se pa sa ki sa?
- you never know - ou pa janm konnen
- Shall we go? Ready? - Eske se pou nou ale? Pare?
- whereas, on the other hand - sou lòt men an, Lè nou konsidere ke
- no problem - pa gen okenn pwoblèm
- for example - pou egzanp
- not bad - pa move
- not at all - pa nan tout
- the more things change... - bagay ki pi chanje ...
- not that great - pa sa ki gwo
- to make a decision - pran yon desizyon

So, you there are some phrases that are quite unique to French. For example, 'n'est-ce pas' does not have a perfectly translated version in Creole. Yet, if you notice, there are many words and phrases in Creole which are deeply rooted in French. So, while you cannot dissociate Creole from French, the uniqueness of Creole is such that simply knowing French will not make you an experienced Creole speaker. You must learn it separately. Learning them together is a great way to make it easy as well as appreciate the commonalities and the individualities of each language.

Conclusion

So, Creole is very close to French and this aspect is not surprising at all considering the fact that Haiti was colonized by the French. This enabled the Haitians to borrow some of the French heritage and culture, especially from the language perspective. The early slaves should be given a lot of credit for developing a new language that has a heritage of its own in today's history books.

Even though the concept of Creole was started with an intention to simply understand what their French masters were saying, the fact that today it a unique language blending French words with the grammar and cultures of multiple African tribes makes those early slaves nothing short of an Oxford scholar. Isn't that what a scholar does; using the available raw materials and data to create something unique, novel, and new that has not been done till now? The fact that these early slaves of Haiti did not even go to school and yet founded a language that is today spoken worldwide talks a lot of their wisdom and intelligence.

So, these brave and strong men picked up a French word like 'Bonjour' with an almost imperceptible sound of 'r' at the end and made it into 'Bonjou' without the 'r' because that is what they heard. They picked up the 'au revoir' from the French (with clearly sounded 'r') and made is 'au rewa,' again because that is what they heard. They used only their hearing skills to make their own communication easier and see what it has resulted in!

Another discerning difference between French and Creole is the finesse that French appears to have while speaking that is absent in Creole. But that only enhances Creole's beauty because the founders created the language with a functional intention and not for any artistic expression. French, on the other hand, has always been a language of finesse and style that poets and litterateurs used to create beautiful poems, ballads, songs, and stories that seem to sing a lullaby as you sleep.

Another example that explains the functionality aspect of Creole is the word uniform. In French, the 'u' at the beginning and the 'r' before the 'm' is clearly discernable to the ear. In Creole, on the other hand, the 'u' becomes an easy-to-say 'i' and the 'r' before the 'm' is not heard at all. So, while the lyrical quality of French may seem missing, Creole still stands tall as a powerful separate language that is not easy to follow and understand even if you knew French quite well.

In fact, it is common for people who know French to not to be able to translate French written works into Creole without first undergoing proper language classes in Creole. The grammar and the formation of sentences that are employed in Creole are more similar to the African languages (the roots of the Creole founding slaves) than to the French language. So, Creole's words might be French but the grammar and culture are African. I would like to end this book by reiterating a famous statement about Creole that is already mentioned in this book and it goes as follows: French is Creole's body whereas Africa is Creole's soul.

I hope this book has intrigued you enough to begin your journey of learning French and Creole. Languages are the ways of humans to articulate their deepest thoughts. If languages did not exist there would have been little difference between human beings and others from the animal kingdom. Words are powerful tools and the more we embrace them the better we get in our relationships with people all around us. Languages have the power to unite. Use this power to bring people closer to each other instead of using it to show seeming differences and separating people from each other.

INSTRUCTION VIDEOS

https://www.youtube.com/user/howtocreole/videos
http://bit.ly/2ueQlt1

Made in the USA
Columbia, SC
24 February 2019